DESIGNS IN SCIENCE

MATERIALS

SALLY and ADRIAN MORGAN

Materials
Copyright © 1994 by Evans Brothers Limited

Facts On File, Inc.
460 Park Avenue South
New York NY 10016

Library of Congress Cataloging-in-Publication Data
Morgan, Sally.
    Materials / Sally and Adrian Morgan.
        p. cm. — (Designs in science)
    Includes index.
        ISBN 0-8160-2985-7 (alk. paper)
        1. Materials — Juvenile literature. [1. Materials. 2.
    Matter.
    I. Morgan, Adrian. II. Title.   III. Series: Morgan, Sally.
    Designs in science.
TA403.2.M67 1994
620.1'1—dc20   93-31722

Facts On File books are available at special discounts when
purchased in bulk quantities for businesses, associations,
institutions or sales promotions. Please call our Special Sales
Department in New York at 212/683-2244 or 800/322-8755.

10 9 8 7 6 5 4 3 2 1

This book is printed on acid-free paper.

Printed by Wing King Tong Co Ltd.

Editor: Su Swallow
Designer: Neil Sayer
Production: Peter Thompson
Illustrations: Hardlines, Charlbury
                David McAllister

Acknowledgments

For permission to reproduce copyright material the authors and
publishers gratefully acknowledge the following:

Cover David Parker / Seagate Microelectronics Ltd. / Science
Photo Library (showing a technician in clean-room clothing
inspecting silicon wafers).
Title page Roberto de Gugliemo, Science Photo Library
Contents page Sally Morgan, Ecoscene
page 6 Michael Holford **page 7** (left) Douglas Dickens, NHPA
(right) Richard Leeney, Ecoscene **page 9** Tweedie, Ecoscene
page 10 (left) Merrell Wood, The Image Bank (right) David
Overcash, Bruce Coleman Limited **page 11** Roberto de Gugliemo,
Science Photo Library **page 12** David Taylor, Science Photo
Library **page 13** (inset) Chinch Gryniewicz, Ecoscene (below)
Robert Harding Picture Library **page 14** Sally Morgan, Ecoscene
page 15 Robert Harding Picture Library **page 16** (top) Sally
Morgan, Ecoscene (below) J.C. Revy, Science Photo Library **page
17** Martin Chillmaid, Oxford Scientific Films **page 18** (top left)
Stephen Dalton, NHPA (inset) Sally Morgan, Ecoscene (below
left) J.C. Revy, Science Photo Library **page 19** (top) Robert
Harding Picture Library (bottom) Sally Morgan, Ecoscene **page
20** (left) Lees, Ecoscene (inset) Eric Soder, NHPA **page 21** Sally
Morgan, Ecoscene **page 22** Anthony Cooper, Ecoscene **page 23**
(top) Sally Morgan, Ecoscene (bottom) Astrid and Hanns-Frieder

Michler, Science Photo Library **page 24** (inset) David
Woodfall, NHPA (bottom) Martin Wendler, NHPA **page 25**
Sally Morgan, Ecoscene **page 26** (left) Sally Morgan, Ecoscene
(main picture, bottom right) Robert Harding Picture Library
page 27 Sally Morgan, Ecoscene **page 28** (left) William S.
Paton, Planet Earth Pictures (inset) Winkley, Ecoscene **page
29** Astrid and Hanns-Frieder Michler, Science Photo Library
page 30 Sally Morgan, Ecoscene **page 31** Robert Harding
Picture Library **page 32** (top) Adrian Davies, Bruce Coleman
Limited (bottom) Walter Murray, NHPA **page 33** (top) B.
Kloske, Ecoscene (bottom) A.N.T., NHPA, (inset) Mark Caney,
Ecoscene **page 34** (top) Robert Harding Picture Library
(bottom) Ayres, Ecoscene **page 35** Prof. P. Motta, Dept. of
Anatomy / University of 'La Sapienza', Rome / Science Photo
Library **page 36** (top) Steve Turner, Oxford Scientific Films
(inset) A.N.T., NHPA **page 38** Tim Thackrah **page 39** Sally
Morgan, Ecoscene **page 40** (left) Sally Morgan, Ecoscene
(inset) Lees, Ecoscene **page 41** Sally Morgan, Ecoscene **page
42** (top) Roy Walker, NHPA (bottom) Sally Morgan, Ecoscene
page 43 (top) Steve Hopkin, Planet Earth Pictures (bottom)
Sally Morgan, Ecoscene **page 44** Lawrence Livermore National
Laboratory, Science Photo Library **page 45** (top) G.I. Bernard,
NHPA (bottom) Fritz Prenzel, Bruce Coleman Limited.

DESIGNS IN SCIENCE
MATERIALS

SALLY and ADRIAN MORGAN

Facts On File

NOTE ON MEASUREMENTS:

In this book, we have provided U.S. equivalents for metric measurements when appropriate for readers who are more familiar with these units. However, as most scientific formulas are calculated in metric units, metric units are given first and are used alone in formulas.

Measurement

These abbreviations are used in this book.

METRIC		U.S. EQUIVALENT	
Units of length			
km	kilometer	mi.	mile
m	meter	yd.	yard
cm	centimeter	ft. or '	foot
mm	millimeter	in. or "	inch
Units of volume			
l	liters	cu. ft.	cubic feet
cm³	centimeters cubed	cu. in.	cubic inches
Units of mass			
g	gram	oz.	ounce
kg	kilogram	lb.	pound
Units of temperature			
°C	degrees Celsius	°F	degrees Fahrenheit

Materials is one book in the Designs in Science series. The series is designed to develop young people's knowledge and understanding of the basic principles of movement, structures, energy, light, sound, materials, and water, using an integrated science approach. A central theme running through the series is the close link between design in the natural world and design in modern technology.

Contents

Introduction

Everything around you, even air, is made up of matter. *Matter* is the name given to anything that has mass. The word *material* is used to describe the type of matter from which something is made. We speak of building materials, for example, or the material used to make clothes. Materials are usually solid, although they can sometimes be in liquid form.

There are thousands of different types of materials. You will already be familiar with many of the most important materials that are found in both the natural and the human-made worlds. These include materials such as wood, cement, concrete, metal, glass, bone and plastic.

The various kinds of material can be grouped together in several ways. An obvious way is to divide materials into those that occur naturally and those that are human-made. For example, wood and cotton are natural materials, but plastic and glass are made by people. However, some materials do not fit perfectly into either category. Paper is one such material; it is made from natural plant fibers but has to be manufactured by people. An alternative is to divide materials into groups with similar physical properties. For example, some materials can be described as strong, some as hard and some as brittle. Different materials may also have a high or low melting point.

The earliest types of materials used by prehistoric humans were those found in the natural world, such as timber, clay, and rock. Early people also used gold that occurred naturally within rocks. This metal could be taken straight from the ground and hammered into shape. More recently, people have learned how to change the properties of materials. This can be achieved by heating a material, by mixing it with other materials or by treating it with chemicals. In such ways, people have learned how to produce completely new substances using materials from both the natural and human-made worlds.

Important decisions have to be made when we choose a particular material to make something. The material has to behave in the right way when a force is applied to it. For example, an unsuitable material may break or bend when we do not want it to. So before a material can be selected,

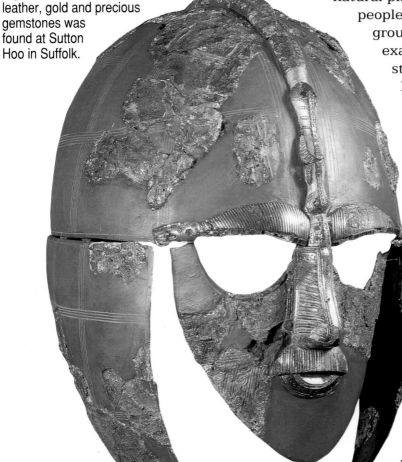

The Saxons, who lived in Britain during the 7th century, used metals, wood and leather to make a wide range of objects. This helmet made of leather, gold and precious gemstones was found at Sutton Hoo in Suffolk.

Beavers use natural materials to build structures such as their dams (below) and lodges. Modern buildings (right) are made from all kinds of materials, some natural and some human-made.

Key words
Composite a material made from more than one substance.
Material the type of matter from which something is made.

a design engineer needs to know how it is to be used. He or she must then calculate how much force it will have to withstand. A material may be used on its own or be mixed with others to form a composite material, depending on the intended use.

This book looks at the wide variety of materials that can be found in the natural and human-made worlds. It looks at the many different materials used by people and other living organisms for building homes and structures. It also studies the ways in which special materials, such as fibers and plastics, are important in our everyday lives.

Important words are explained at the end of each section, under the heading of **Key words**, and in the glossary on page 46. You will find some amazing facts in each section, together with some experiments for you to try and some questions for you to think about.

Atoms and elements

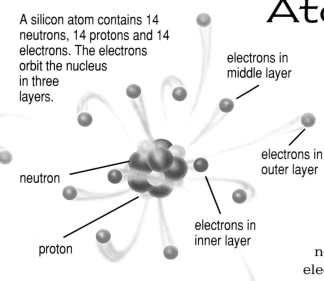

A silicon atom contains 14 neutrons, 14 protons and 14 electrons. The electrons orbit the nucleus in three layers.

electrons in middle layer

electrons in outer layer

electrons in inner layer

neutron

proton

Materials are made from tiny particles called atoms. Atoms are so small that it is impossible to pick up a single atom and look at it. It is not even possible to see atoms using the most powerful electron microscopes. Despite being unable to see individual atoms, scientists have been able to find out a lot about them.

Atoms are made up of three main types of smaller particle – protons, neutrons and electrons. The heaviest part of an atom is the nucleus, found in the middle of the atom. The nucleus contains protons, which have a small positive charge, and neutrons, which have no charge at all. Surrounding the nucleus is a cloud of tiny electrons, each one of which carries a small negative charge. Normally an atom contains an equal number of protons and electrons, so that the positive and negative charges cancel one another out and the atom is neutral. The largest naturally occurring atom is uranium, which has 92 electrons. Uranium can be used to make plutonium, the most toxic substance known to humankind. Hydrogen is the smallest atom, with only one electron. Ten million million million million atoms of hydrogen would weigh only 1.7g (0.0595 oz.).

Atoms can exist on their own and in groups. Groups of atoms joined together are called molecules. Molecules can then join together to form elements or compounds.

! *An atom is so tiny that four billion sodium atoms would fit on the period at the end of this sentence.*

Elements

An element is a substance that is made of only one kind of atom. For example, copper is made up only of copper atoms, therefore copper is an element. There are 92 different chemical elements that occur naturally. People have been able to make a further 12 elements artificially, mostly by controlled nuclear reactions.

An element cannot be broken down into a simpler substance. For example, the element oxygen is made of oxygen atoms and therefore cannot be broken down into a smaller and more simple element. Elements are the "building blocks" from which all matter is constructed.

Elements can be joined together to form compounds. For example, water is made up of the two elements, oxygen and hydrogen. A substance like wood, however, is a much more complex compound. It is made from long chains of carbon, oxygen and hydrogen atoms. A compound is made by combining two or more elements chemically. The resulting substance usually has very different properties than the elements from which it is made. Water, which is a liquid, behaves very differently than either oxygen or hydrogen alone (both of which are gases). It is possible to make millions of compounds from the 104 different elements.

! *95 percent of the mass of our body is made from just four elements – oxygen, hydrogen, carbon and nitrogen.*

The many different seaweeds, marine animals and rocks in this rock pool are made of compounds formed when elements bond together.

Chemical reactions

A substance can be changed by heating it, adding water to it or mixing it with another substance. When any of these things are done, changes may be observed. For example, bubbles of gas may be produced, the color of the substance may change, heat energy may be taken in or given off or a new substance may be produced. When a new chemical substance is produced, the change is called a chemical reaction. A chemical reaction is difficult to reverse. For example, chemical changes take place when you fry or boil an egg. The white of the egg becomes hard and whiter in color and the yolk becomes much firmer. These changes are impossible to reverse because of the chemical reaction that has occurred.

When a chemical reaction takes place, the atoms within one substance (either in an element or compound) react with atoms in another substance. A new compound is formed when different atoms are bonded together. A bond is an attraction between two atoms that holds the atoms together. It is a little like gluing two atoms together. For example, when the metal sodium (an element) is heated and placed in a jar of chlorine gas (an element) the sodium burns with a bright flame. A white substance, sodium

Is the burning of a piece of wood a chemical or physical change?

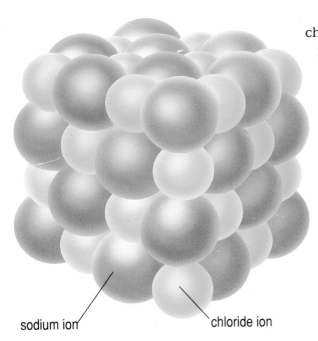

A crystal of sodium chloride (common salt) contains a regular lattice of sodium ions (a sodium atom minus one electron) and chloride ions (a chlorine atom plus on electron) bonded together.

sodium ion   chloride ion

chloride, is formed on the sides of the jar during the reaction. The heat produced during the reaction enables sodium atoms to bond to chlorine atoms and form a new compound. Another common example of a chemical reaction is the burning of carbon in air. Fuels such as coal, oil and gas contain carbon atoms. When carbon is burned in air a new compound is formed. This is called carbon dioxide.

Bonds can be broken as well. It is possible to break the bonds between atoms in one compound to form two smaller compounds. For example, a molecule of glucose (a simple sugar) consists of six atoms of carbon, 12 atoms of hydrogen and six atoms of oxygen. Glucose can be broken down into two smaller compounds – water and carbon dioxide. This series of reactions, jointly known as respiration, takes place in living cells. It is a very important chemical reaction since a lot of energy is released during this process. This energy is used by living organisms to grow, move and reproduce.

The chemical reactions described above are different from physical changes. Sugar can be dissolved in water, but the sugar molecules do not react chemically with the water molecules. It is possible to separate the sugar from the water again. Physical changes are usually relatively easy to reverse and have important uses.

A metal undergoes a physical change (left) when it is heated to its melting point. While the metal is in a molten state, it can be molded into a new shape. The many colors of fireworks (below) are produced from a chemical reaction when different elements burn in air.

Large-scale atomic structures

A crystal of quartz is made of silicon dioxide. Pure quartz is colorless and transparent, but when impurities are present it is colored.

Some materials are made up of simple molecules, while others have a more complicated structure. For example, sand is a very common substance that is made from a complex framework of atoms. Sand is mainly composed of a chemical compound called silicon dioxide. Silicon dioxide is produced when atoms of silicon are bonded to atoms of oxygen. The atoms are arranged into a rigid structure, held in place by many bonds rather like scaffolding. This very stable structure means that sand is hard and is difficult to melt. It is therefore an important building material, found for example in concrete and cement.

Metals, too, have large atomic structures. The atoms in a metal are packed tightly together in a regular pattern. They are all held in position by bonds. The tight packing makes metals very dense materials. They usually have high melting points because it takes a lot of heat energy to break the bonds between the atoms. However, the bonds in metals are quite flexible and can be stretched. Metals can therefore be bent into different shapes without breaking the bonds. They are described as malleable materials, meaning that they can be bent or hammered into new shapes without losing any of their strength. Metals can also be mixed with other substances to form alloys. Alloys have different properties from the original metals. For example, pure iron is too soft to be useful for building things. If the iron is melted and a little carbon mixed into it, the iron becomes much harder and stronger. The new material is an alloy, known as steel (see page 29).

The atomic frameworks of some materials are large enough to allow other substances to fit inside. This changes the way in which the material behaves. Clay (see page 27) is a very good example of this change in behavior, for the presence or absence of water greatly affects its properties. When it is wet, clay is very slippery and easy to mold. However, when it is dry it is brittle and crumbly. This change occurs because clay, is made of sheets of atoms. In clay, these sheets are made up of atoms of silicon, oxygen, aluminum and hydrogen, which are all mixed together. When water is added to the clay, the water molecules are trapped between the sheets. The water molecules provide a lubricating film that allows the sheets to slide easily over one another. If the clay is dried in the sun or a human-made kiln, the water molecules evaporate and the sheets cannot slide anymore. The clay then becomes hard and brittle.

Key words

Atom the smallest particle of a chemical element that can exist alone and still be that element.
Bond a linkage or attraction between two atoms.
Compound a substance made by combining two or more elements.
Element a substance made up of atoms of just one type.
Molecule a group of atoms bonded together.

There is a very rare fourth state of matter called a plasma. This state can be produced by heating a gas to an extremely high temperature, causing the atoms to break apart. The sun is a ball of plasma.

Hot air is less dense than cold air, so a balloon filled with hot air (heated by burners) will rise up into the sky.

States of matter

Matter can exist in one of three states – solid, liquid or gas. It is possible for materials to be changed from one state to another. Most materials that are in common use are either in the solid or liquid state.

Metal and wood are examples of materials that occur in the solid state. Solids make very good building materials because they have a fixed state that is difficult to change. A force has to be applied to a solid to change its shape. The atoms within the solid are packed closely together, held in position by strong bonds. Although each atom is in a fixed position, the bond can be stretched. So the atoms cannot move about, but they can vibrate if sufficient energy is applied.

Liquids can flow freely and change shape easily. They have a fixed volume, but take the shape of their container because molecules within liquids are not strongly bonded to one another. For this reason, liquids are not normally used as structural materials. However, they are commonly used as lubricants to reduce the friction between two solid materials in contact with one another. Oil, for example, is used as a lubricant in car engines. Surprisingly enough, glass is also an example of a liquid. Glass looks as if it is a solid, but it is really a supercooled liquid. This is a special state in which the atoms of a liquid move so slowly in relation to one another that the liquid behaves as if it were a solid.

Gases have no fixed shape or volume, so they spread out to fill the available space. This means that a small amount of gas released into a large room will quickly spread throughout the room. There are no bonds holding the molecules of gas to one another, so the molecules are free to move about very quickly in a random way, often colliding with each other. Even if a gas is placed in a container, it will still spread out to occupy all the available space. If enough pressure is applied to a gas, it can be squashed or compressed into a very small space. Divers therefore use cylinders of compressed air to breathe under water. Tires also contain "squashed" air. An inflated tire is full of air at three times the pressure of the air outside. The earth's atmosphere contains many different gases, including nitrogen, oxygen and carbon dioxide. The only reason why these gases do not drift off into space is because the molecules of the gas are individually attracted to the earth by the force of gravity. Space itself is a huge vacuum where there are no gases.

Changing state

Diamond is the hardest natural substance known to humankind. It has a very high melting point of 3550°C (6422°F) and boils at 4832°C (8729°F).

Why are salt and sand spread on roads when ice or snow is expected?

Natural materials can change state. Lava is a hot liquid that escapes from volcanoes during an eruption (main picture). When lava cools it solidifies and forms a lava rock that is very light in weight (inset).

When a substance is heated, that is, given heat energy, the atoms within it move about more rapidly. When a solid is heated, the atoms within it vibrate more and more rapidly. Eventually, if there is enough energy, the bonds holding the atoms in place break. When this happens, the solid melts and becomes a liquid. If even more heat is applied, the atoms move faster still and they eventually break away from the other atoms in the liquid. The liquid then evaporates and forms a gas. This happens most rapidly when the temperature of the liquid reaches its boiling point. However, liquids can evaporate slowly even below their boiling point. We rely on this process of evaporation for our clothes to dry. Certain animals, including humans, use evaporation to remove excess heat from their bodies when they sweat (see page 20).

Many materials can exist in all three states, depending upon their temperature. A good example of such a substance is water. Below 0°C (32°F), water is frozen and in a solid state that we call ice. If water is heated so that its temperature rises above 0°C, the ice melts to become a liquid. If the liquid is heated still further to 100°C (212°F), it will eventually come to the boil and turn into water vapor, the gaseous state of water. These changes of state work in reverse as well. If the gas cools below its boiling point of 100°C, it will condense and become a liquid once again. Similarly, if the liquid is cooled to below its freezing point of 0°C, it will turn back to ice.

A change of state can be very helpful when using materials. For example, when metals are in their molten state they can be molded into new shapes. As they cool, they retain their new shape. A change in state also occurs during the manufacture of plastics (see page 22). Some types of plastic become soft when heated and can be molded into a new shape.

EXPERIMENT

States of matter

In this experiment you will examine the movement of atoms in different states. You will need a square lid from a box, or a shallow tray, some pieces of cardboard and a large number of marbles or small polystyrene spheres, and some tape or glue.

1 Divide the lid into three sections, as shown in the photograph, using thin strips of cardboard. Fix the cardboard into place with the tape or glue.

2 Fill the small space completely with marbles.

3 Put the same number of marbles into each of the other two areas.

4 Gently move the tray back and forth so that the marbles move around. Do not tilt the tray. Notice how the closely packed marbles cannot move very much. This resembles the positioning of atoms in a solid. The marbles in

the next area can move further, but they still bump into each other a lot. This is like the atoms in a liquid. Finally, the marbles in the largest area are able to move about independently. This is similar to the way in which atoms move in a gas.

? *Why do some movies and rock concerts use dry ice as a special effect?*

Some substances do not have a liquid state at all. Instead, they turn from a solid directly into a gas. This process is known as sublimation. Solid crystals of iodine, for example, will turn directly into a purple vapor when they are heated, without first melting. Carbon dioxide behaves in the same way. If carbon dioxide gas is cooled to -55°C (-131°F), it turns directly into a solid, known as dry ice. The change in state from solid to gas requires a lot of heat energy, and this energy is taken from the surrounding air. Dry ice is therefore a good refrigerant and so is used to keep things cool.

Gels

A gel is a special state of matter between a liquid and solid. It can be produced by mixing a solid with a liquid. The solid forms a flexible network within which the liquid is prevented from flowing around freely. If a gel is pushed or squeezed gently, it will move out of shape, but it will regain the original shape if the pressure ceases, rather like rubber (see page 40). However, if more force is applied, it can be made to flow like a liquid.

A familiar example of a gel is mucus, a slimy organic material. Mucus is used in the natural world to lubricate and protect. Mucus in humans is produced by cells in the mouth, nose and throat, especially when the body is infected with cold or flu. Fish are covered in a protective mucus layer. This slippery layer helps fish to swim through the water and makes them very difficult to catch with bare hands!

Snails produce mucus to help them move along the ground.

Grease and petroleum jelly are gels. They act as lubricants, for example in engines, stopping moving parts from rubbing. This prevents energy being wasted through friction. Many of the "non-drip" paints and glues on the market today are gels. Many foods contain natural gels. The Jell-O that we eat contains a gel called gelatine. The gelatine, usually colored and in powdered form, is mixed with hot water. The gelatine melts, then the mixture is placed in the fridge to cool. As it cools, the Jell-O becomes solid. However, if you push a finger into the Jell-O it changes shape. Jams, too, contain natural gels called pectins. Pectins are found in many fruits, especially the citrus fruits. Pectins cause the jams to become firm as they cool. However, jam is neither solid nor liquid. It is just firm enough to stick to a spoon but runny enough to spread on bread. Researchers are developing many new and exciting uses of gels as part of a range of "smart" materials (see page 45).

Key words

Gas a substance containing molecules that move freely and fill the available space.

Gel a substance that is part solid and part liquid.

Liquid a substance with fixed volume but variable shape.

Solid a substance that has a fixed shape that is difficult to change.

EXPERIMENT

Making a gel

Flour is often used in cooking to thicken sauces and soups. It can be used in this way because flour contains starch that forms a gel when heated in water. The gel is produced when long chains of starch form a network that traps water. In this experiment you will investigate the effect of altering the amount of flour you add to the water. You will need 200g (7oz.) of flour (any type), 100 cm³ (a little more than 3oz.) cold water, a small saucepan, a wooden spoon, a tablespoon and a stove.

Warning: Using the stove only with an adult present, be careful and tie back long hair out of the way.

1 Place one heaped tablespoon of flour in the saucepan and add the cold water. Stir well so that the flour is mixed into the water and there are no lumps.

2 Heat the mixture slowly over a low heat, stirring all the time.

3 Remove from the heat once the mixture starts to bubble. How thick is the gel? Does the gel drop off the spoon? Allow the gel to cool for 10 minutes. What happens as the gel cools?

4 Repeat the experiment using two tablespoonfuls of flour, then three and finally four. What differences do you notice?

Polymers

Polymers are very large molecules made from many sub-units called monomers. The monomers are joined together to form a long chain, the polymer, which always contains carbon, hydrogen and oxygen. There is a huge range of both natural and human-made polymers. They are found in every living organism. Cells, for example, contain natural polymers such as protein (see below). Human-made plastics such as polystyrene and polyvinyl chloride (PVC) also contain polymers.

Two important groups of natural polymers are proteins and carbohydrates. Protein is a polymer made from monomers called amino acids that have bonded together into very long chains.

Fibrous proteins have structural functions. Other proteins, called globular proteins, form a ball-like shape. They are usually involved in cellular functions, such as respiration (see page 10).

Carbohydrate polymers include starch and cellulose. Starch is vital to the survival of plants. It is built up from monomers of glucose, a type of sugar. Plants store starch in their leaves and roots to be used as a future source of energy. When energy is needed, the starch is first broken down into glucose. The glucose is then broken down to release the energy contained within it. Cellulose is also a polymer made from glucose. It is used to make the cell walls around every plant cell. Cellulose is a strong material, which gives the cell its regular shape and protects it.

Human beings eat a lot of protein and carbohydrates. Polymers are too large to pass through the walls of the gut and blood vessels, so they need to be digested first, that is, broken down into monomers. When you eat a piece of bread, for example, the starch is broken down by special chemicals called enzymes into a sugar called maltose. Enyzmes are natural catalysts, substances that begin or increase the speed at which chemical reactions take place. Starch would break down into maltose without enzymes, but over several days rather than in seconds. The maltose is then broken down into glucose, which is small enough to pass directly into the bloodstream.

It is only recently that we have learned how to make synthetic (artificial) polymers. Synthetic polymers first appeared about 100 years ago, but were very rare and expensive. During the 1950s, technology improved and crude oil, the raw material from which many synthetic polymers are made, became widely available. This meant that synthetic polymers could be made very cheaply.

Polymers can be divided into two main groups. These are called fibers and plastics.

Proteins are made from many amino acids joined together to form a chain, rather like these beads.

This plant cell is packed with spherical starch grains.

Fibers

? *What happens to woolen garments if they are washed in very hot water? Why?*

! *There are 150 million sheep in Australia. Altogether, they produce enough wool each year to stretch from the earth to the sun 8,000 times.*

Fiber is the term used to describe a long, thin strand of material. There are many different sources of fiber. Some, such as cotton and coconut fiber, come from plants. Others, such as wool, come from animals. There is also a wide range of human-made, synthetic fibers such as nylon, rayon and polyester. Sometimes fibers are twisted together to form stronger strands. Woolen yarns, which are used to make textiles such as fabric, are examples of twisted fibers.

Our own bodies contain many types of fibers, each with their own specific functions. Animal hair, nails, hooves and horn are all made from a fibrous protein called keratin. In keratin, the chain of amino acids is twisted into a spiral rather like the cord of a telephone. Each human hair is made of many such chains of keratin. This spiral structure makes hair surprisingly strong and elastic. Wet hair can stretched quite a lot and yet will spring back into shape.

Mammals are unique in the animal kingdom in having developed hair to insulate them from the cold. It is often specially colored for camouflage. Sheep and goats have been bred for their wool for thousands of years. Their coats are needed for protection and insulation during the winter months. In spring, the coat is shed so that the animal does not overheat in the summer.

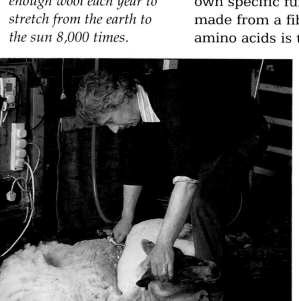

Although sheep still molt naturally in spring, domesticated sheep are sheared. The fleece stays together while it is being cut, because each hair is naturally curly and interlocks with neighboring hairs.

Silk

Silk is a remarkable natural fiber. Many animals are able to produce silk. The most common are spiders, but it is the silkworm that is farmed to make silk on an industrial scale. Although many human-made fibers similar to silk are available, none completely reproduces the look and feel of natural silk.

Silk is made by the caterpillar of the silkworm moth. The caterpillar spins a cocoon of silken threads to protect itself in its "resting" or pupal state. It undergoes many changes in this state to emerge finally as a fully formed adult. It wraps a long thread around itself many times until it is completely enveloped in silk. This single, unbroken thread of silk may be up to 2 km (1.25 mi.) in length. In order to harvest the silk, farmers place the cocoon in water to loosen the silken threads. This allows the whole cocoon to be unwound as a single fiber.

! *The finest kimonos are made from the silk of over 3,000 silkworm cocoons.*

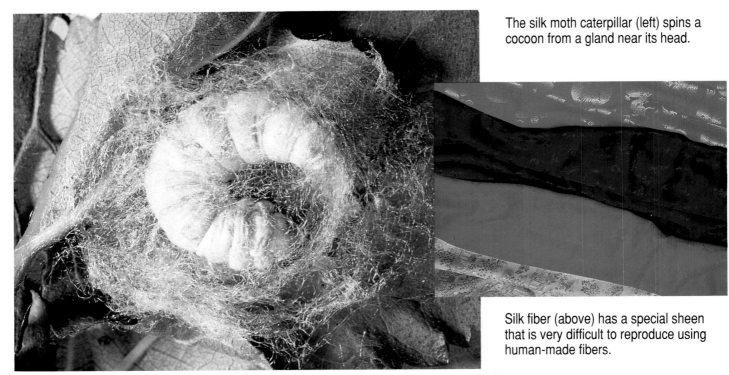

The silk moth caterpillar (left) spins a cocoon from a gland near its head.

Silk fiber (above) has a special sheen that is very difficult to reproduce using human-made fibers.

Female spiders also spin silk, to make their webs and construct shelters. Spider silk is strong but very flexible. It can withstand a relatively large flying insect, such as a butterfly or bee, flying into the web. Scientists have been trying to learn how the spider makes the liquid silk turn into a solid fiber. If they can discover the method, they will be able to manufacture a useful form of synthetic silk. For example, such a silk would be strong enough to replace the Kevlar fibers in bullet–proof jackets.

Plant fibers

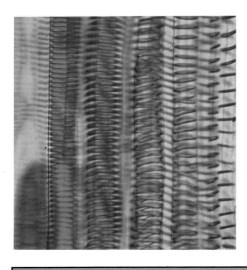

The blue horizontal lines in this "false color" photograph of a plant cell are empty "drain pipe" cells called xylem vessels.

Plants produce a huge variety of fibrous material. Flowering plants produce xylem, a strong tissue running all the way from the roots, through the stem, to the leaves. The xylem tissue is responsible for conducting water and minerals around the plant. It contains dead cells called xylem vessels, whose cell walls are strengthened with lignin. Lignin is a tough material that is the main constituent of wood (see page 24). However, the lignin stops oxygen from entering the cell, so xylem cells die when the lignin is laid down in the cell walls. Once the cells are dead, the end walls drop out, leaving a column of cells that resembles a tiny drain pipe. Xylem vessels form tough fibers that are very difficult to break.

Plants also produce fiber cells. These are similar to xylem vessels, for they are also dead cells with walls containing lignin, but fiber cells are much shorter and have tapering ends. These cells are laid down in areas of the plant where extra support is needed, such as in the stem and the leaf.

Flax, sisal, jute and hemp are all types of fiber made from

To harvest the cotton, the bolls have to be removed from the top of the cotton plant either by hand or machine.

plant stems. The plant stems are cut and soaked in water. The outer covering, or epidermis, is removed and the inner fibers separated out. The inner fibers may then be twisted together to form string or rope, or they may be woven together to make a flat sheet of fabric. For example, fibers of flax are woven together to produce linen, a tough cotton-like fiber. Sisal fibers are between one and two meters (3'4" to 6'8") in length and ideal for making twine, rope, nets, hammocks and some types of carpet.

One of the most familiar and widely used natural fibers is cotton. Cotton fibers are attached to the seeds inside the cotton "bolls" that have developed from the flowers of the cotton plant. The cotton boll has to be picked off the plant and the seeds then pulled off the cotton fibers. The fibers must then be untangled so that they all lie in the same direction. The cotton can then be spun into a single, long thread. Today, the cotton can be mixed with some human-made fibers, such as polyester, to improve the fabric's strength.

Most natural fibers, with the exception of silk, are too short and weak to be used in their raw state. However, several shorter fibers may be spun together into a single longer and stronger thread. The natural fibers have to be cleaned and untangled to produce a clean and straight fiber known as a sliver. Several slivers at a time are fed between rollers that stretch and twist the fibers into a coarse thread. This thread is then wound on to a bobbin to be woven into fabric.

? *Cotton has many uses, not just for clothing. How many different uses can you think of?*

Synthetic fibers

Scientists have developed a wide variety of synthetic fibers. The atomic structures of fibers, and the chemical processes needed to produce them, are now so well understood that it is possible to design new fibers for particular uses. Synthetic fibers behave in a similar way to natural fibers, but they tend to be stronger.

Rayon is a typical human-made fiber that is actually made from the plant material cellulose (see page 16). The cellulose is extracted chemically from plant material, including trees such as spruce, balsam and hemlock. The wood is chipped and then digested in a acid solution. The lignin is dissolved by the acid and can be

Cellulose comes from wood pulp and part of the process is very similar to making paper. This dried cellulose has a texture rather like blotting paper.

removed. The remaining pulp is whitened using bleach and then washed. The cellulose is rolled into a long sheet that is later cut into smaller pieces. Cellulose has many uses. It may be treated to become liquid rayon, a material that is often called viscose. The liquid can be extruded (stretched out) into thin fibers for use in such things as tire reinforcement, textiles, teabags, and disposable diapers. Cellophane is also a product of cellulose. It is used in kidney machines to filter the blood and is found in tape and food wrappings. It is also an ingredient of face creams, ink and instant mashed potato!

Oil is a common base material from which many synthetic fibers are made. One of the earliest synthetic fibers made from oil was nylon. Nylon is useful because it is strong, flexible and light in weight. Unlike cotton and wool, it will not shrink in hot water and does not rot. There are many hundreds of types of nylon. For example, Kevlar is a particularly tough material that cannot be cut with scissors. It is used in bullet-proof vests (see page 18). Another very common use of nylon for clothing occurs in the manufacture of tights and stockings.

Many modern fabrics are now designed to meet specific needs. For example, stretch fabrics such as Lycra and Spandex have been developed for use in leisure and sports clothing. These fabrics cling to the body but still allow sweat to evaporate from the skin. They are particularly useful for athletes, swimmers and cyclists because they do not billow out and catch the wind or water, and so slow the wearer down.

Many fabrics need to be waterproof. The process of waterproofing relies on a property of water called surface tension. Surface tension is caused by the attraction of water molecules for other water molecules. They cling together, forming a

The best waterproof fabrics contain tiny holes to let water vapor from the skin escape into the air.

Waterproofing is particularly important for water birds. This duck is using its beak to straighten out its feathers and spread oil over them.

Testing fabrics

When choosing a fabric for an item of clothing or for upholstery, it is important to think about how the fabric is to be used. Designers have to consider whether a fabric needs to be waterproof, fire-resistant, comfortable or long wearing. In this experiment you will test a range of fabrics to see how waterproof they are and whether they can withstand being rubbed. You will need some samples of different fabrics (such as PVC, pure cotton, polyester/cotton mix, wool, and nylon), a jam jar, a rubber band, water and a rough stone or piece of sandpaper.

1 Cut out a small square of fabric and stretch it across the top of the jam jar. Fix it in place with the rubber band.

2 To test for waterproofing, slowly drip water onto the surface of the fabric. Does the water stay on top or soak through? How quickly does it soak through? How much water can you add before the water starts to drip through?

3 Now gently rub the fabric with your rough

stone or sandpaper. Repeat the waterproofing test to see whether roughing up the surface of the fabric changes its ability to repel water in any way.

4 Rub the fabric again, this time more vigorously. How long do you have to rub to produce a hole in the fabric?

5 Repeat the experiment using the other samples. Compare your results.

sphere. The water stays on the surface of the fabric in big droplets.

Many animals waterproof their own feathers or fur. Birds produce an oily secretion from a gland called the preen gland. They rub this oil over all of their feathers using their head and feet. The oil waterproofs their feathers and helps to maintain good insulation.

Even the surface of human skin is waterproof. Our skin is composed of many layers of cells. The outermost layer consists of flattened, dead cells rich in keratin (see page 17), which waterproofs the cells. Further waterproofing in the human skin comes from a secretion called sebum. Sebum is an oily substance produced by glands within the skin at the base of each hair. The sebum spreads along the hair and over the skin where it forms a thin waterproof layer, preventing water from entering. Human skin is a thin, flexible and waterproof outer covering. Like a synthetic membrane, it has tiny pores to allow sweat to reach the surface of the skin.

For safety reasons, it is very important that some fabrics resist fire, especially where they are used in the home or for clothing. Animal hair does not burn easily and tends to smolder rather than burn, but many synthetic fabrics, such as nylon, do catch fire easily. These fabrics are said to be combustible. Plant fibers, too, are combustible. Modern fabrics are often treated with chemicals to make them fire-resistant.

Select three or four different garments from your wardrobe. From what material is each made? What makes the material suitable for that garment?

Plastics

There are at least 100 kg (220 lbs.) of plastic in every modern car, and this amount is steadily increasing.

Plastics are used more and more in our everyday lives for an enormous range of purposes, from toys and buildings to clothes and furniture. Plastics are long-chain polymers (see page 16) made from oil. They are cheap, light and easy to shape and color. They are often very tough, yet flexible. Today, new plastics can be designed to order with specific properties.

There are two main groups of plastics: thermoplastics and thermosetting plastics. Thermoplastics can be softened and melted by heating. Thermoplastics melt and change shape because, when heat is applied, the polymer chains in these plastics are free to slip past each other. Old thermoplastics can be re-melted and molded into new objects.

Thermosetting plastics, by contrast, do not soften when heated. Instead, they stay hard and rigid. If they are heated to a high enough temperature, they will start to burn. These plastics are used in such things as electrical fittings, which must not melt if they get hot. Thermosetting plastics do not soften because the polymer chains are cross-linked. Neighboring chains have bonds between them, so they cannot move freely or slide around.

Some polymers can be used both as fibers and as molded plastic. For example, nylon (see page 20) is used as a fiber in textiles and toothbrushe bristles, but it can also be molded into plastic bearings and gear wheels. When it is used as a fiber, the chains of polymer are extruded (drawn out) and untangled. When it is used as a plastic, the chains remain tangled together in a cross-linked structure (see page 40 on rubber).

Our homes contain many types of plastics. Can you identify the thermoplastics and thermosetting plastics in this photograph?

Biodegradable plastics

Plastics are a very common material in modern products because they are relatively cheap to make and have such a wide range of useful properties. However, most human-made polymers have one major disadvantage over natural polymers – they do not rot or decay. Natural polymers such as cellulose and cotton are biodegradable. This means that these materials will quickly decompose if left outside where bacteria and fungi can feed on them and cause them to decay naturally. On the other hand, a piece of plastic left outside will remain unchanged for many years. This produces major waste disposal problems. Many landfill sites contain large amounts of non-biodegradable plastic. Burning plastics is not a good solution, since many plastics are made from chemicals that produce toxic gases when burned.

Why might biodegradable materials take longer to break down in winter?

EXPERIMENT

Investigating biodegradability

In this experiment you will bury some materials and then dig them up a few weeks later. You will discover which materials are biodegradable and whether or not the size of the material affects the rate at which it breaks down.

You will need four different materials such as newspaper, cabbage leaves, a disposable plastic cup and an eggshell. You will also need a knife, scissors, spade, some sticks or canes, a pair of rubber gloves, a few labels and a marker pen.

1 Collect your four materials. Part of each material should be buried in one large piece, for example a large leaf of cabbage, half a sheet of newspaper, half of the plastic cup and half an eggshell. The other part of your material should be broken up into small pieces, which should be buried together. Chop up your cabbage, tear the paper, cut up your plastic cup and break up your eggshells.

2 Go into your garden and dig eight small holes in the soil. The holes should be close together and about 10 cm (4 in.) deep. Place each material in a different hole and cover it again with soil. Mark the place where you buried each material with a stick. Make a note on the label saying what is buried there and tie it to the marker stick.

3 Leave the materials in the soil for a couple of weeks. If you do this experiment in winter, you will have to leave them for at least a month, ideally two.

4 Wearing a pair of rubber gloves, dig up your materials again and examine them. Throw everything away when you have finished and wash your hands.

Have any of the materials been broken down? How much is left of each? Are there any differences between the large pieces of material and the ones that were torn up into smaller pieces?

Fortunately, scientists have learned how to make some plastics biodegradable and are looking for ways of making others break down naturally. One promising approach is to use genetically engineered bacteria that will feed on the plastic. One type of biodegradable plastic contains a small quantity of starch that can be digested by soil bacteria. This causes the plastic to be broken down into tiny particles that mix into the soil.

We need a large number of landfill sites because so much of our waste material is made of non-biodegradable plastics.

Key words
Biodegradable capable of being broken down by natural processes.
Fiber a long, thin thread of material.
Plastic a human-made material made from oil-based chemicals
Polymer the large molecule made from a number of sub-units.

Building materials

An enormous range of materials is used for building structures, both in the natural and human-made worlds. The best building materials are strong, durable (long lasting) and easily obtainable.

Wood

People have used wood for constructing shelters, for fencing, for making wheeled carts and for weapons for thousands of years. Wood is a remarkably versatile material, with properties that vary widely depending on the tree from which it is obtained. There are two main categories of wood: hardwoods and softwoods.

Hardwood comes from flowering trees such as the oak and beech tree. The woody tissue of a hardwood tree is composed mostly of xylem tissue containing lignin (see page 18). These trees produce a dense, hard wood that is very long lasting. It rots extremely slowly, so it is ideal for building. Hardwoods, such as mahogany and teak come from tropical rain forests. The wood has rich colors ranging from deep yellow to deep red, is very hard and contains an attractive grain (pattern of wood).

Softwoods come from coniferous trees (those with cones) such as the pine and spruce. The cells making up the xylem in these trees are different from those in a hardwood tree. The cells are much shorter and not as tough as those of hardwoods.

Mahogany and other hardwoods such as teak have been used to make high-quality furniture for hundreds of years. The trees are removed from the rain forests where they grow (above) and taken to a sawmill, where the trunks are cut up into planks (right).

Fresh wood contains too much water so it has to be left outside to season. What happens to the water?

One important feature of wood as a material is that it is a renewable resource. Softwoods can be planted and then harvested 10 or 20 years later, though hardwoods take considerably longer. The rapid growth rates and straight trunks of the softwood conifer have made it a valuable commercial crop in the United States, Canada and North European countries. Coniferous trees are a conical shape, unlike hardwood trees, and they have few side branches. This makes the wood easier to process at the sawmill.

Very little of the wood is wasted; even the sawdust can be used. Small off-cuts of wood are chipped and used for wood pulp to make paper or cellophane (see page 20). Larger pieces may be sawn into strips, glued together and sandwiched between slices of veneer (a thin strip of finer wood) to make blockboard. Plywood is a very strong wood material since it is made from several thin sheets of wood glued together. The grain of the wood is laid alternately in different directions. This makes the sheet strong and prevents the plywood from warping.

A number of chemicals can be extracted from wood if it is heated or treated chemically. When wood is heated, it releases oils and resins that can be further treated to form a range of products such as tar, ethanol, creosote and turpentine. Pine trees, in particular, release a lot of resin. All of these substances have many uses. Turpentine, for example, can be used to thin oil-based paints. In many developing countries, charcoal (a black porous carbon substance produced from wood) is a common fuel for cooking.

The sawmill is often some distance from the forests, so the logs are floated down rivers in huge rafts.

Paper

Paper and cardboard are made from wood pulp and a mixture of different chemicals. The wood pulp, which is rich in cellulose, is mixed with water, chalk and other chemicals to form a thick, wet paste. This paste is then spread over a moving conveyor belt with holes in it. The holes let the water drain from the pulp, allowing the fibers to lock together to form a layer of wet paper. The paper becomes stronger as more water is removed. The ideal water content of the finished paper is six percent. The wet paper is then

In the first stage of making paper, the wood pulp is mixed with water and chemicals.

Excess water is drained off the pulp.

After passing through the ovens, the dry paper is wound on to rollers.

The finished paper can be cut into sheets of the required size.

squeezed through a series of rollers and passed through ovens to dry. It is then wound on to a huge roller, ready to be cut into pieces of paper of whatever size is required.

The quality of the paper depends on the length of the cellulose fiber in the pulp. Wood pulp provides very long fibers that mat together to form a strong paper. New paper can also be made by recycling used paper. However, the fibers of recycled paper tend to be shorter and this affects the quality of the product. Usually a small amount of wood pulp will be mixed with the recycled paper pulp. The quality of recycled paper varies depending on its intended use. Poorer quality recycled paper can be used for paper towels and toilet paper while the better quality recycled paper can be used for writing paper and even for books. Paper is not made only from wood. Different plant fibers can be used to make papers of varying texture, appearance and strength.

Some animals make paper too. Wasps make their nests from paper, unlike the honeybee, which constructs its comb from wax. Worker wasps forage for wood that they then chew, mixing it thoroughly with their saliva. This produces a pulp that the wasps place in position with their forelegs. The paper then hardens on exposure to air.

! *40,000 liters (10,400 gal.) of water are needed for one tonne (1.1 tons) of paper!*

? *Can you think of six different uses for paper?*

The rough paper that makes up the wasp's nest is strong and extremely light in weight. This allows wasps to build quite large structures.

Examining paper

The strength and absorbency of paper depends on the length of fibers used to make it. In this experiment you will test the strength and absorbency of some papers. You will need a

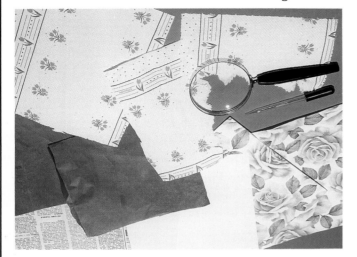

selection of different papers, such as recycled paper, writing paper, newspaper and paper towels, an eye dropper, colored water or ink, scissors, a magnifying glass, a notebook and pen.

1 Cut up your paper samples into squares of the same size, ideally 20 x 20 cm (8" x 8"). You will need two squares of each sample. Carry out the following tests on each type of paper.

2 Test each type of paper for strength. How easy is it to tear? Using your magnifying glass examine the fibers along the torn edge of the paper. Are the fibers long or short? Are they easy to see? Note your findings.

3 Now test each sample for absorbency. Fill your eye dropper with colored water or ink. Take a sample of paper and drip a few drops of water onto the surface of the paper. Watch what happens carefully. Does the water sit on top of the paper or does the paper absorb it? How far does the water spread across the paper? Repeat the test with another sample. Take care to drop the same amount of water onto each. Note your findings and compare them. How might you make these tests more accurate?

Clay

Clay is used to build homes both by people and animals. Clay is made of tiny particles of rock less than 0.002 mm (0.00008 in.)in size. When it is moist, clay is very flexible and can be easily shaped and molded, usually into bricks or tiles. As clay dries, the moisture content is lost, and it hardens into a rigid solid, keeping its shape (see page 11). This baking process can happen naturally in hot climates. For example, termites build huge nests of clay that rise several meters above the ground. The clay bakes hard in the hot sun of the tropical countries where the termites live.

In Africa, Central America and the southwestern states of the United States, many houses are still made with clay walls. Clay bricks or wood form the main structure, and then more clay is packed over this framework and allowed to dry in the sun. In Mexico and the United States, this kind of structure is known as an adobe house. As natural resources such as wood are becoming scarcer and other materials are becoming more expensive, adobe building techniques are being re-evaluated for modern houses. The clay walls are reinforced with steel to make them rigid and

The first bricks, made from clay and reinforced with straw and dried in the sun, were made 8,000 years ago in Mesopotamia.

strong. In areas where there are hot days and cool nights, such as in the southwestern United States, these clay walls can provide energy savings of 30–40 percent. These savings occur because the clay absorbs heat during the day and releases it at night, helping to maintain a comfortable temperature.

Clay is also used by a number of different animals to make their nests. House martins make cup-shaped nests of clay under the eaves of houses. The most tricky problem when building these structures is how to attach the mud to the vertical wall. This problem is solved by a very clever method of construction. House martins position the mud while rapidly vibrating their heads, in an action very similar to a cement mixer. This causes the clay to become "non drip," or thixotropic, preventing it from dripping when it is applied.

House martins (above) build distinctive mud nests under the eaves of houses and barns. Houses made using adobe (mud) are cool during the day (right) and warm at night. It is an ideal material for building in hot desert areas.

Metals

Of the 92 naturally occurring elements, 81 are metals. The strength, hardness and malleability of many metals (see page 13) make them very important structural materials. Metals also have high densities, however, so they are heavy for their size, which can cause problems when building large structures. Metals are also good conductors of heat and electricity.

Scientists describe many metals as being chemically active. This means that they will readily react with other elements or compounds. There are also a few unreactive metals, such as gold and platinum, which are often used for ornamental purposes such as jewelry. Metals can be mixed to form alloys that usually have greater strength and are harder than the individual metals from

More than 10 percent of the earth's crust is made of aluminum.

Zinc is a blue-white metal, used chiefly to galvanize iron and to make alloys such as brass.

The smelting of iron ore takes place in a blast furnace.

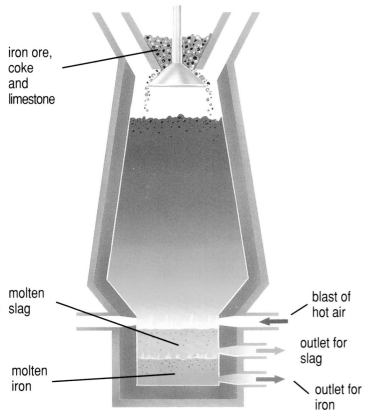

iron ore, coke and limestone

molten slag

molten iron

blast of hot air

outlet for slag

outlet for iron

which they are made. Brass, for example, an alloy of copper and zinc, is stronger than either copper or zinc. In a pure metal the atoms are all the same size and they can slide over each other. The metal can be made to change shape. In an alloy the atoms are of two different sizes and they cannot slide over each other so easily.

Most metals are reactive. They do not occur naturally in the ground, since they would react with water and other chemicals in the soil or rock. Instead the metals are found in compounds called ores. The ores have to be quarried or mined. The metal is then extracted from the ore and purified. Gold, an unreactive metal, does occur in pure form in the earth, as gold nuggets.

Iron is one of the cheapest and most important metals. It has to be extracted from iron ore by a process called smelting. This takes place in a blast furnace. Iron ore, coke and limestone are fed into the top of the blast furnace while hot air is blown in at the bottom. The carbon in the coke burns in the air. This produces a lot of heat energy, which allows two very important chemical reactions to take place. The carbon reacts with the oxygen in air to produce carbon monoxide gas. This carbon monoxide reacts in turn with the oxygen contained within the iron ore. This reaction forms iron and carbon dioxide. The iron is liquid, or molten, in the high temperatures of the furnace, so it flows to the bottom of the furnace where it can be poured off. The limestone helps to remove any impurities in the iron ore. It combines with the impurities left in the ore and floats on top of the molten iron. This mixture is called "slag." It can be drained off separately and used for various purposes, such as making roads.

The iron extracted from iron ore is called pig iron. It contains about four percent carbon (due to heating with the coke), which makes the pig iron very hard but brittle and so of limited use. However, if the carbon content is reduced to less than one percent, the iron is turned into an alloy, known as steel. Steel is a very tough, strong metal with many useful applications.

Examining corrosion

Corrosion is a chemical reaction between a metal and another chemical, usually oxygen (either in water or air). The surface of the metal is oxidized in this process and forms a new chemical substance. For example, iron forms iron oxide, known to us as rust. This experiment will examine the rusting of iron nails to discover what encourages rusting and what slows it down. You will need six small jam jars with lids or test tubes with stoppers, six long, shiny, iron nails, a kettle, some salt and some oil.

1 Place one nail in a dry jar and replace the lid.
2 Fill the second jar two-thirds full of tap water and drop in one nail. Replace the lid.
3 Boil some water in the kettle for about five minutes. This will remove any dissolved air from the water. Let the water cool and then carefully fill the third jar two-thirds full of water. Drop a nail into the water and then carefully add some oil so that a layer of oil forms on the surface of the water. Replace the lid of the jar. The nail in this jar will be in oxygen-free water.
4 Add a little water to the fourth jar and position the nail in the jar so that it is half in

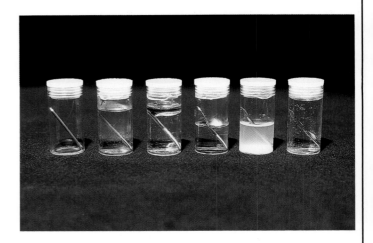

and half out the water. Replace the lid.
5 Put a little water in the fifth jar. Add a teaspoon of salt to the water. Position the nail half in the water and replace the lid.
6 Completely fill the sixth jar with tap water. Dip a nail into some oil so that it is completely covered in a layer of oil. Place the oiled nail in the water.
7 Leave all the jars for at least a week, then examine each nail.
Which jars contain rusty nails? Did any treatment stop rusting? How might iron and steel be treated to prevent corrosion?

Glass and ceramics

Glass at the bottom of old window panes is much thicker than the glass at the top. This is because glass is a supercooled liquid and over many years the molecules in the glass slowly move downward.

Glass has been used by humans for much longer than most people realize. In fact, the first glass is thought to date back to 3000 B.C., when it was used as a glaze on pottery and stone by the Sumerians of Mesopotamia and the ancient Egyptians. Glass is a remarkable material, being very stiff and resistant to scratching, yet transparent. Glass is made up of 60 percent sand (silicon dioxide), 20 percent soda lime and 20 percent limestone. The chemicals are mixed and heated to 800°C (1472°F), at which temperature the mixture becomes molten and glass is formed. It can then be molded into sheets, bottles and other shapes before cooling back into its supercooled state (see page 12), in which it becomes rigid again. Very few chemicals can attack glass, so it can even be used for storing concentrated acids. It will not conduct electricity (except when molten), and it is also a poor conductor of heat. Glass expands when heated, as do metals, but borosilicate glass (known more commonly by its trade name, Pyrex) hardly expands at all,

Molten glass can be formed into many shapes. Bottles, glasses and other containers are made by blowing air into the middle of some molten glass.

! *Glass made from just sand and soda is soluble and can be used to make soluble glass pills containing drugs or vitamins.*

even when very hot. Because it is less likely than ordinary glass to break when rapidly heated and cooled, Pyrex is ideal for cooking.

The flat sheets of glass used in window panes are made by a special method. While the glass is still molten, it is poured onto the surface of a bath containing molten tin. It is then allowed to cool slowly. This method prevents any contaminants from coming into contact with the glass in the early stages of cooling. This helps to avoid distortion in the finished pane of glass.

Ceramics, like glass, are hard, brittle materials. Ceramics such as china are made from clay in a process very similar to that used to make bricks. Ceramics are brittle, so the number of applications for these materials is limited. In contrast, many plastics are soft and flexible, so engineers are trying to combine plastics with ceramics to produce new materials, known as organo-ceramics. The new materials would combine the properties of plastics and ceramics and be resistant to both scratches and impacts. Such new materials would be ideal for use as car windshields, lenses and artificial bones. In the future, organo-ceramics may be used for rebuilding teeth and bones or in slow-release pills for drugs. The drug would be encapsulated within organo-ceramic layers. As the digestive system slowly eats these layers away, the drug is released gradually in small doses.

Expansion and contraction

One problem encountered in using materials for building, or for use at different temperatures, is that many will expand when they are heated and contract when they are cooled. The change in size is usually very small, but it can be significant over a large area, for example in bridges or runways. To avoid this problem, large concrete and metal structures contain built-in gaps to allow the material to expand safely.

When certain materials are heated, the heat energy causes the molecules within the material to vibrate and take up more space. The molecules are gradually pushed further apart, and the material expands. As the material cools, the molecules vibrate less rapidly and take up less space, so the material contracts again.

Key words
Corrosion a chemical reaction caused by air, water or other chemical on the surface of a metal.

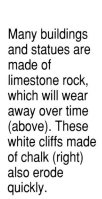

Calcium-rich materials

Calcium is a very common element occurring in many rocks and in the bodies of living organisms. When calcium is combined with other substances such as carbonates (a salt containing carbon and oxygen), it becomes a very useful structural material. Calcium is an important element in both natural and human-made structures.

Calcium carbonate occurs naturally in chalk and limestone rocks. It can be quarried straight from the ground and is employed in a wide variety of different industries. It is used in road construction, in the manufacture of glass (see page 30) and for liming (neutralizing) acidic soils. Calcium carbonate can also be changed into "slaked" lime by heating it and adding water. Slaked lime is used in building mortar and also for making pottery.

However, calcium carbonate is very susceptible to attack by acids. Like all carbonates, it reacts chemically with acid to form carbon dioxide. Since rain water is naturally slightly acidic, it slowly dissolves limestone rock. This has an important effect on the landscape of chalk and limestone areas, forming cliffs, valleys and even underground cave systems. Unfortunately, the same effect happens to limestone buildings and statues. In heavily industrialized areas, the rain water is now even more acidic due to atmospheric pollution. As a result, the rate at which the limestone is dissolving has rapidly increased. The environmental hazard of acid rain is caused mainly by industrial waste gases, such as sulfur dioxide. When this gas dissolves in rain water it forms a weak solution of sulfuric acid.

Many buildings and statues are made of limestone rock, which will wear away over time (above). These white cliffs made of chalk (right) also erode quickly.

Shells and skeletons

Many marine invertebrates, such as coral-forming animals and mollusks, cannot move around. They have to rely on currents in the sea to bring their food to them. Such invertebrates are described as sessile. To protect their soft bodies from predators and wave action, they either bury themselves in the sea bed or live inside tubes or shells. The main component of such tubes and shells is calcium carbonate. Mollusk shells come in many different shapes and sizes, ranging from the single spiral shell of the periwinkle to the domed single shell of the limpet and the huge hinged shells of the giant

Pipi shells, like all other shells, are made from crystals of calcium carbonate embedded in layers of protein.

clam. These shells contain crystals of calcium carbonate that are embedded in layers of protein (see page 35 on bone). New layers of shell are added as the animal grows inside. Each new layer of the shell projects outward from the older layers. This produces a series of concentric growth lines that are visible on the outside of the shell. The outermost layer of the shell is chemically different from the others and it protects the lower layers from being dissolved by weak carbonic acid in sea water.

Coral animals are related to the larger jellyfish and sea anemones. They live in colonies and each individual coral animal builds an external calcium carbonate skeleton to support and protect its soft body. When the animal dies, its soft body decays, leaving behind the hard skeleton. Other coral animals build their skeletons on the old ones. In time, the coral gets larger and larger. Some corals, known as gorgonacean corals, contain protein as well as calcium carbonate in their skeletons. This makes the skeleton more flexible, allowing it to bend in response to pounding waves or strong currents.

Sponges are another form of marine animal, often found on coral reefs. They are very simple animals in evolutionary terms, but they can grow quite large so they need a strong skeleton. Most sponge skeletons are formed from tiny needles of calcium carbonate embedded in a protein called spongin (made by sponges). These natural sponges were used for bathing for many years because the skeleton would hold a lot of water that could easily be squeezed out. Today natural sponges have been replaced by human-made sponges made from foam rubber, which has similar water-holding properties.

Sponges (above) are supported by a calcium carbonate skeleton embedded in protein. Coral animals (right) build an external skeleton made of calcium carbonate.

Single-celled animals called protozoa also possess shells rich in calcium carbonate. The skeletons of one particular group of protozoa, called the foraminifera, have formed much of the chalk rock found all over the world. When these tiny marine animals died, their bodies sank to the bottom of the sea bed and became covered in mud. Although the soft parts of the cells decayed, the hard skeletons, rich in calcium carbonate, remained. Layers of these skeletons built up over time. Eventually, pressure from the top layers of sediment crushed the skeletons in the lower layers and, over millions of years, chalk rock was formed.

Cement and concrete

Cement and concrete are human-made materials manufactured from common materials such as limestone, clay, sand and gravel. Cement is made by mixing powdered chalk or limestone with clay and water and heating it in a kiln. The substance that results is called clinker. The clinker is then mixed with gypsum or calcium sulphate and crushed to a powder, a dry form of cement. When this powder is mixed with water and sand, a mortar forms that can be used to bind substances together. However, when the cement mortar hardens, it is easily broken in the hand. It will shatter if dropped since the mortar is brittle. Scientists are trying to improve the strength and the usefulness of cement, so that it could become an alternative to metals and plastics. Some progress has been made following an examination of the microscopic structure of cement. This showed that cement mortar contains a lot of air holes, many of which are quite large. If the air holes are made smaller, the cement becomes stronger. Experiments have shown that the strength of the mortar can be improved simply by mixing the water, sand and cement more carefully, thereby letting less air enter the mixture. Chemicals can also be added to stop particles clinging together in lumps and allowing the cement to mix more thoroughly. These improvements in cement technology mean that this material may be used for a greater variety of jobs in the future.

Concrete is made by mixing sand, gravel and cement together with water (above). It can be reinforced by pouring the concrete over a network of steel rods (right).

How many different uses of concrete do you know?

A natural cement can be found in our mouths. Our teeth are held in place in the jaw by fibers and a form of cement.

Concrete is a strong material that wears well and can withstand heavy weights and extremes of weather. It is ideal for building roads and bridges. Concrete is made by mixing sand or gravel with cement and water. The strength of concrete comes from the large particles of sand and gravel. However, concrete alone has limitations, so it is often made stronger by reinforcing it with metal such as steel. Concrete can be reinforced relatively easily, by being poured over a network of steel rods. It can also be "pre-stressed" in the factory. This process means that steel rods are stretched by great weights before the concrete is poured over the rods and allowed to set. When the tension on the steel rods is released, the rods try to return to their previous length. However, they are unable to do so because of the concrete. The rods compress (push on) the concrete and so strengthen the whole structure. Pre-stressed concrete is suitable for a wide range of engineering structures.

Bones and teeth

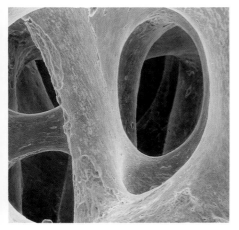

Bone is a natural composite material made of a matrix of calcium and phosphate together with tough fibers of collagen.

Fish, amphibians, reptiles, birds and mammals are collectively known as vertebrates. They all have a complex internal skeleton, or endoskeleton. These skeletons are made from two tough materials: cartilage and bone. The skeleton of a shark is entirely composed of cartilage, while those of mammals contain both materials. Cartilage is a more flexible, fibrous material, whereas bone is much stronger and is a better material for use in larger skeletons, such as those of vertebrates that live on land.

Bone is an example of a composite material, since it is made up of a number of different substances that all contribute to its characteristics. Bone is an unusual building material in that it can repair itself. Although we may think of bone as an inert material, it is, in fact, living. If you cut living bone, it will bleed. However, the living cells in bone only make up a small proportion of the whole material. The bulk of bone is made up of a white background material called the matrix. The matrix is secreted by living bone cells. Blood vessels, nerves and the bone cells themselves are all embedded within the matrix, which also contains the mineral salts calcium and phosphate and many tough fibers of collagen, an example of a fibrous protein. The calcium phosphate gives bone its strength, while the collagen fibers provide a degree of elasticity. This means that bones are able to flex a little without breaking.

Each bone has a slightly different job to do and therefore each bone needs different properties. The amount of mineral present in the bone greatly affects its strength and flexibility in the same way that the carbon content of steel affects its strength (see page 29). The tiny bones in the ear are called ossicles. They are designed to transfer sound energy from the outer ear to the inner ear without losing any energy. In fact, the ossicles are arranged so

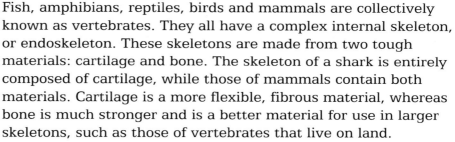

Weight for weight, bone is as strong as reinforced concrete.

Elephants' ivory tusks (above) are flexible so that they do not break during fighting. They contain a lower mineral content than the stiff, strong bones of the foal (right). Many young mammals have to be able to stand up and run within minutes of birth.

? *The teeth of mammals are designed to suit their diet. How are the teeth of a carnivore, such as a dog or cat, adapted to feeding on meat?*

! *Ivory is a form of enamel. The hardest and densest ivory is found in elephant tusks, which can reach several meters in length and more than 45 kg (99 lbs.) in weight.*

that they magnify sound by approximately 22 times. The ossicles have to be stiff and they cannot afford to bend. However, they do not have to be very strong as they are protected by the skull. The ossicles are therefore quite brittle and are 70 percent mineral by volume. In contrast, a bone such as the antler of a deer has to be tough since it is used in fights, especially during the mating or rutting season when male deer fight over females. Antlers have a much lower mineral content (just 50 percent) and more protein, which means they are less brittle and much more flexible. Leg bones have an intermediate amount of mineral since they need to be both strong and stiff. The amount of mineral and protein in bone changes depending on the age of the individual mammal. There is a difference between the bones of human adults and children. Children's bones are more flexible than those of adults, so children suffer from fewer broken bones. However, when children's bones do break they tend to split rather than break cleanly. This is called a "greenstick" fracture. As the child becomes older, the amount of mineral in the bones gradually increases. This enables the bones to support the adult weight. Unfortunately, many older people, especially women, suffer from a disease called osteoporosis in which the bone becomes porous and brittle. It is caused by the loss of calcium from the bone.

Not all young mammals have flexible bones. Some mammals, notably horses and antelopes, need to be able to get up and run with their mother within minutes of birth. To enable them to do this, the young are born with bones that contain more minerals and so are quite stiff and strong.

Fiberglass, known more correctly as glass-reinforced plastic, is a human-made material very similar to bone. This material consists of very stiff but brittle glass fibers embedded in flexible plastic. The glass fibers provide the strength, like the minerals of the bone matrix, while the plastic provides elasticity, like the collagen fibers of bone. This combination of substances in fiberglass produces a composite material that can be bent without shattering. Even though a crack may start in one glass fiber, it will stop when it reaches the plastic matrix, which prevents the crack from continuing through the whole material. A good example of fiberglass in use is the pole vaulter's pole. The pole can be bent almost in half and is strong enough to enable the

Bones in space

Since Yuri Gagarin, the first cosmonaut, was launched into space in 1961, scientists have discovered that our bodies quickly adapt to conditions of near-weightlessness. In a spacecraft orbiting the earth there is almost zero gravity, so the astronauts float freely and their bodies no longer have to support their own weight. Unfortunately, the human body is badly affected by weightless conditions. The muscles quickly atrophy (waste away). If the astronauts have spent many weeks in space, their bodies are often unable to support their own weight when they return to earth. In fact, an astronaut can lose up to 25 percent of the mass of the main weight-bearing muscles on only a nine-day mission. The loss of this muscle is mostly in the thighs and calves, the muscles that support our bodies. However, the muscle can be quickly regained once the astronauts return to earth. Vigorous exercise reduces the rate of muscle loss but does not stop it. Human bodies also discard calcium in space, often at a rate of 0.3–0.4 percent per month. Astronauts who spend several months on board space stations therefore also develop brittle bones. Some bones, such as the heel bone, were found to lose as much as 5 percent of its original calcium content per month. This loss of calcium is called osteoporosis (see page 36).

!

Astronauts may be several centimeters taller when they return to earth as their spines have not had to support their body weight for a period. One astronaut gained over 6 cm (2.5 in.) in height.

vaulter to spring up from the ground, yet it is also extremely light.

The teeth of mammals are ideal for biting and chewing. They have evolved over millions of years into the perfect shape for their purpose. Each tooth is composed of layers. The outer layer is enamel, one of the hardest known natural substances. Enamel is very dense and brittle, being composed mainly of calcium phosphate. Beneath the enamel is a layer of a substance called dentine, which contains fibers of protein as well as calcium phosphate. Dentine is a bone-like material and is more flexible and softer than enamel. The properties of enamel and dentine are different for a good reason. When biting, the enamel has to

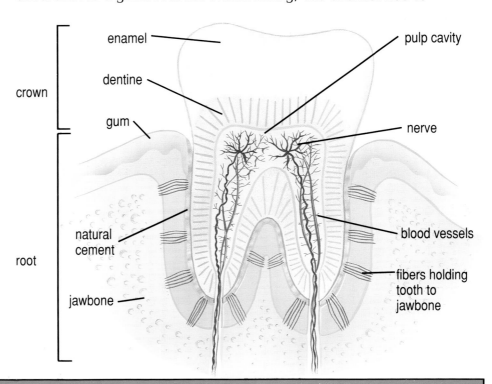

The tooth is in two main parts – the crown, which is above the gums, and the root, which is embedded in the jawbone.

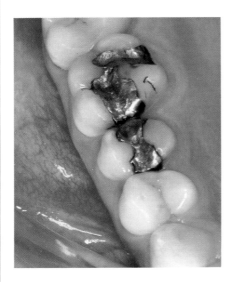

Examining teeth

You will need a small mirror, a notebook and pencil and some friends and family to help you.

1 Use a mirror to help you examine your own teeth. How many teeth do you have? An adult will have a full set of 32 teeth, but children do not get their full set until their late teens or twenties when their last teeth, the wisdom teeth, break through.

2 You have four different types of teeth, incisors, canines, premolars and molars. Try to identify the different types of teeth in your mouth. Are any missing in your mouth?

3 Do you have any fillings? There are several types of filling, for example the silver colored mercury amalgam (see photograph), gold and the latest acrylic polymers, which look like natural enamel. Acrylic polymers bond with the surface of the tooth and look better than amalgam fillings.

4 Examine the teeth of your friends. Do they have any fillings?

5 Examine the teeth of a parent or older relative. Does he or she have any fillings? Does he or she have 32 teeth?

Do older people have more fillings than young people? If so, can you think why?

Why is it important to clean one's teeth after a meal?

withstand a large force acting downward. The dentine below gives a little when this force is applied, cushioning the force and so preventing the brittle enamel from breaking.

Natural materials rot or decay when exposed to certain chemicals or conditions, just like iron and steel. Enamel is vulnerable to attack by acids, and the long term result of this attack is tooth decay. Everyone has millions of bacteria in their mouth that are not harmful under normal conditions. These bacteria tend to collect in the grooves of the teeth and between the teeth and the gums. However, the remains of sugary food collect in the same places and provide energy for the bacteria. The bacteria release acid as they digest the food. The bacteria and acid form a sticky covering over the teeth, known as plaque. The acid starts slowly to dissolve the enamel, and if it is allowed to continue will eventually attack the dentine below. Decay spreads quickly through dentine because this substance is much softer and contains living cells that are highly sensitive to the acid. Once the decay reaches the pulp cavity in the middle, the nerves will be affected, causing pain. The bacteria may even reach the blood vessels in the pulp cavity and produce an infection. Dental decay can be prevented by brushing teeth regularly and especially by flossing between the teeth. Fluoride toothpastes help to resist acid attack because the fluoride is absorbed by the enamel. This helps to increase the natural strength of the enamel.

If dental decay takes place, the decayed part has to be removed and the space in the tooth filled by an artificial material with similar properties to the material it replaces. A number of different materials have been used to fill teeth. The new material must be capable of being shaped, so that the biting surface of the tooth remains the same. The mouth is a warm, wet, often acidic environment that causes many metals to corrode. The most common filling material for teeth, mercury amalgam, is an alloy of mercury, silver, tin, copper and zinc. It is mixed only when needed, so that it is soft and can be shaped easily. On exposure to air it hardens rapidly and expands slightly to give a tight fit. Other materials used in dental fillings include gold, which is soft and can be shaped easily. However, gold is expensive and never becomes as hard as mercury amalgam. More recent materials include acrylic polymers, but these are still being developed.

Growth and repair

Growth is a characteristic of all living organisms. For example, flowering plants continue to grow throughout their life. In contrast, humans grow rapidly during the early stages of their life but stop growing once they reach adulthood. Many natural materials that make up living organisms can even repair themselves if damaged. Broken bones will knit together again. Teeth of rodents, such as rats and mice, grow throughout their life. As a tooth becomes worn down through eating, it re-grows. Some animals are able to re-grow entire limbs and other parts of their body. Lizards often lose their tails. The tail is designed to break easily, enabling the animal to escape from a predator. The tail then slowly regenerates (grows back). Starfish, too, are able to regenerate lost arms.

Human-made materials do not have the ability to repair themselves. Once a steel or concrete bridge has been constructed, the shape and size of the bridge cannot alter. If the metal starts to corrode, the corrosion must be treated so that no further damage occurs. However, the damaged metal is not able to regrow. It is these types of features that scientists are trying to incorporate into new human-made materials (see page 45).

The tail of many lizards is designed to break easily so that the animal can escape if caught. The tail slowly re-grows.

Key words
Bone a natural composite material capable of repairing itself.
Concrete a human-made composite material ideal for building roads and bridges.
Regeneration regrowth of a new organ or tissue.

Rubber and glue

Rubber and glue are examples of materials that are rarely used on their own to make things. However, they are frequently found in composite structures because of their unique properties. Rubber, for example, is used to provide suspension mounts for the engine in a car and to protect passengers from jolts. Rubber also gives bicycle tires their springiness and grip. Glues can be used wherever it is necessary to join two different materials together. Its uses range from sticking the flap of an envelope down to gluing an artificial joint in place.

Rubber

! *In 1876 a British explorer smuggled 70,000 rubber seeds out of Brazil and took them to Kew Gardens in England. Until this time, Brazil had a monopoly on rubber since the rubber tree was found only in South America.*

Rubber is an extremely useful material. It is a natural polymer (see page 16) made from a white liquid called latex. Latex is produced by plants, most notably the rubber tree. In a method called "rubber tapping" spirals of bark are cut from the tree. Latex drips through the cracks.

The attraction between the long polymer chains in rubber is weak, allowing them to slide over one other when a force is applied. However, the attraction is strong enough to make the chains tend to spring back into shape when the force is released. Heat makes the polymers slide even more freely, allowing the sticky liquid rubber to be poured into special shapes. However, such natural rubber does not keep its shape well, especially in hot weather.

To help rubber retain its shape, it can be

Rubber trees (left) produce latex from their damaged bark. The latex drips from the cut and is collected in a cup. Car tires (above) are made from rubber that has been hardened by adding elements such as sulfur.

Rubber and spaghetti!

In this experiment you will examine the way spaghetti strands slip over each other, imagining that the strands of spaghetti are polymers of rubber. You will need 20 long pieces of spaghetti, a little oil, a large saucepan, a plate, two forks, a colander, some water and the use of a stove.

Warning: Use the stove only with an adult present and be careful near the stove and picking up the saucepan of hot water. Tie long hair back before you begin.

1 Half fill your saucepan with water and heat it on the stove. Add the spaghetti to boiling water. Cook for 7 minutes.

2 Drain the hot water away in the colander. Using the forks, remove approximately half the spaghetti. Cool it on the plate.

3 Rinse the remaining spaghetti with cold water in the colander. Add 2 teaspoons of oil to this spaghetti and mix it in with a fork. Leave the spaghetti to cool.

4 After about 10 minutes, when both portions of spaghetti are cold, try to pull the strands apart. What effect has the oil had?

The portion without the oil should be more difficult to separate because the strands of spaghetti will have stuck together. This is similar to the way cross-links form in cured rubber. The portion with the oil should be easier to separate. The oil prevents the spaghetti strands from sticking together as in natural rubber.

strengthened by cross-linking the chains. This means that they do not slide over one another so easily. Cross-linking is usually carried out by heating the rubber and exposing it to chemicals in a process called curing. More recently, the strength of rubber has been further increased by the use of a material called carbon black. This improves the strength and resistance of rubber.

By far the most useful feature of rubber is its elasticity. The material can be stretched and will return to its original shape when released. Rubber tends to get more elastic as the temperature increases, but at very low temperatures it becomes brittle and can even shatter when droped on a hard floor. If too much force is applied, the polymer chains will become fully extended and will then suddenly snap. If the rubber has been kept stretched for a considerable time it may not return to its original shape. For example, if you blow up a balloon and leave it inflated for a day, the rubber will become permanently deformed. When you release the air from the balloon, it does not deflate to its original size.

Why do racing cars use tires made of soft rubber?

Glue

Glues, or adhesives, are an important material in our everyday lives. They are often liquid and sticky when they applied to a substance, but they harden and become a solid that locks objects together. Glues are substances found in both the natural and the human-made worlds.

Many animals and plants make sticky materials that behave in a similar manner to glues. A well-known example is the garden spider. The female spider makes a web of silk threads (see page 18). The inner part of the web where she waits is not sticky like the outer part. Insects are trapped when they fly into the sticky threads.

The mussel is a marine animal that attaches itself to rocks. The mussel is quite difficult to remove from a rock because threads from the lower part of its shell are stuck to the rock by a strong natural glue. This glue is made by the mussel itself.

Resin is a runny substance that is produced by trees, especially conifers. It is exuded from the trunk of the tree in

Mussels are firmly attached to rocks so that they are not washed away by waves.

(see page 18)

EXPERIMENT

Making glue from milk

In this experiment you will make a natural glue using milk. This glue was used thousands of years ago by the ancient Egyptians. Objects made using this glue have been found in Egyptian tombs, still intact after all the centuries in between. You will need 500 cm³ (17 oz.) of skimmed milk, a little baking soda (sodium hydrogen carbonate), some vinegar, a saucepan, a glass bowl and an old spoon.

1 Pour the milk into the saucepan and add 100 cm³ (about 3.4 oz.) of vinegar. Heat the milk gently until lumps form.

2 Pour the milk into the bowl and let it cool. You should then find a large lump of rubbery material at the bottom of the bowl, covered by a layer of watery liquid.

3 Pour off the watery liquid and mix the solid with 25 cm³ (.85 oz.) of water and a teaspoon of baking soda. A chemical reaction takes place that produces a glue. This glue can be used to stick all sorts of things together – test it on two sheets of paper.

Super-glue is so good at sticking to skin that doctors sometimes use it for attaching skin grafts.

small, sticky drops. Insects often get stuck in these drops.

Many carnivorous plants rely on sticky substances to trap their insect prey. These plants usually live in nutrient poor areas, such as peat bogs, and must rely on insects to provide them with essential minerals. The sundew plant has leaves covered in sticky tentacles. Any insect landing upon the leaves becomes trapped. Glands in the tentacles then secrete digestive fluids to break down the soft body of the insect.

There are two types of human-made glue – solvents and polymerizers. Solvents are substances, usually liquid, that are able to dissolve other substances. Water is a very common solvent since many substances dissolve in it, such as sugar. Solvent glues consist of a solid dissolved in a solvent. When the glue is spread, the molecules of solvent evaporate into the air, leaving just the solid on the item to be glued. A common example is the glue found on the back of stamps. This glue is made of gum, a natural substance made by plants. Gum becomes sticky when moistened with water. When the stamp is placed on an envelope, the water evaporates and the gum locks the paper and stamp together.

Polymerizing glues do not need solvents. Instead, they consist of two compounds, a monomer and a hardener. When the monomer is mixed with the hardener, it turns into a polymer and becomes hard. The hardening process is called curing. The newly formed polymer binds the glued surfaces together. However, the polymer must not form in the tube, as it would stick to the sides, so the glue is sold in two tubes, one containing the monomer and the other the hardener. The hardener often contains another chemical called a catalyst (see page 16), which causes the reaction that forms the polymer to work more quickly. Without the catalyst, the glue would take a long time to harden. Epoxy resins, such as Araldite, use a hardener together with a catalyst. Cyano-acrylates, known as super-glues, use water as a catalyst. When super-glues are spread on a surface, they come into contact with air that naturally contains some water vapor. Super-glues harden extremely rapidly. They are very powerful and must be used with great care.

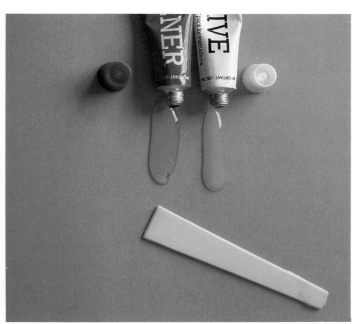

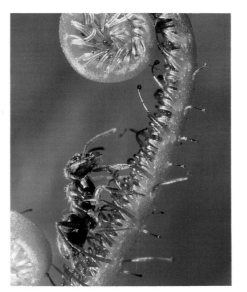

The sundew plant produces a natural glue to trap small insects (below right). Epoxy resins are very powerful, human-made glues (above).

Key words
Catalyst a substance that starts a reaction or makes it proceed faster but does not actually take part in the reaction.
Glue a material that will bind two surfaces together.
Rubber an elastic material made from latex.
Solvent a liquid in which a particular substance will dissolve.

The future

We can be certain that the future will see many exciting developments in the science of materials. The most promising new technologies are those involving composite materials, such as ceramics and organo-ceramics and those in biologically engineered materials.

The very latest plastic is so resistant to heat that it can withstand temperatures of 2700°C (4892°F) – the heat of a nuclear explosion. The properties of this plastic have been demonstrated by coating an egg with the plastic and then putting the egg in the flame of a welding torch. The egg remained uncooked and undamaged and could be handled as soon as the welding torch was switched off. The applications for this new plastic have yet to be explored fully, but they are expected to range from the fireproofing of furnishings to the possible protection of space vehicles during re-entry into the earth's atmosphere. The friction between the space vehicle and the atmosphere during re-entry produces a lot of heat and so the vehicle is covered in special insulating tiles. It would be much simpler just to cover the vehicle in a layer of the new plastic.

Packaging material of the future may be made from the ultra-lightweight SEAgel. This material is so light that it is supported by bubbles of air.

Balsa wood is a strong and very lightweight wood, but supplies are dwindling, so replacement materials with similar properties are being developed. One of the most interesting potential replacements is called Safe Emulsion Agar Gel or SEAgel. It is made from kelp extract (kelp is a type of seaweed). SEAgel is a solid material, but it is almost as light as air. It weighs so little that it would float away in a gentle breeze. Because it is made from kelp, it is biodegradable and is also safe to eat. Its uses will probably include packaging, refrigerator insulation and time-release drug capsules.

Composite materials will become far more common than they are today, especially in the car and aircraft industries. New motor parts will soon appear that make extensive use of composite materials, including fiber-reinforced metal alloys known as metal matrix alloys. These will help to make high performance cars lighter and stronger. A car manufacturer, Honda, will soon start to line the cylinders of the engine of its Prelude car with an aluminum alloy, reinforced with short lengths of ceramic fiber. The ultra-hard ceramic fibers will improve the wear and heat resistance of the metal cylinder liners, allowing them to be much thinner than at present. Less heat energy is lost to the cylinder block, thereby increasing the efficiency of the engine.

The shell of the abalone is very tough, just like the protective armor of tanks.

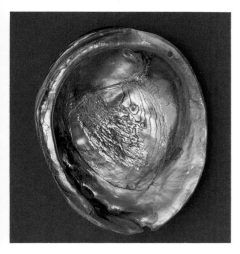

This photograph of Sydney, Australia, shows both natural and human-made materials. Living organisms are made of materials that can react to stimuli, change shape and even repair themselves. Human-made materials in general do not, although those of the future may be able to do so.

One of the most exciting areas of research today is into "smart" materials. These are human-made materials that can respond to stress and other physical changes, just as living materials do. Much of the research involves study of the way natural materials behave, in an attempt to reproduce this behavior in artificial materials. For example, scientists have studied the structure of the abalone, a marine mollusk with a heavy protective shell. The shell is a composite material with small crystals of calcium carbonate embedded in a polymer, rather like mortar joining chalk bricks. This design of the abalone shell was shown to be so strong that a similar design was adopted for tank armor.

A new and interesting type of smart material is the polymer gel. These gels can change chemical energy into kinetic energy by bending or expanding as their chemical properties are changed. Smart gels have already been designed that are able to make a model wing flap and a model fish swim, acting rather like artificial muscles.

Smart concrete will be able to repair itself in a way similar to how bone repairs fractures. Smart concrete contains plastic fibers filled with an anticorrosion agent. This concrete may soon be able to stop cracks from spreading and to prevent steel reinforcing rods from corroding. Any corrosion of the steel that takes place within the concrete will cause the outer coat of the fiber to dissolve. This in turn releases the anti-corrosion agent that stops the corrosion spreading. Other fibers inhibit cracking. Smart concrete could even be strengthened further by adding adhesive-filled fibers to the material. If a crack forms, the fiber would be broken and the adhesive released, thus sealing the crack immediately.

Developments in smart materials show how important it is for scientists to study living organisms. New ideas can be introduced into human-made designs that have their basis in the natural world. The process of natural selection ensures that only successful natural designs survive. Therefore, scientists are wise to look at natural designs that have passed the test of time.

Glossary

alloy a mixture of two or more metals.
atom the smallest particle of any chemical element that can exist alone and still be that element.
biodegradable broken down by natural processes.
bond a linkage or attraction between two atoms.
bone a natural composite material able to repair itself.
carbohydrate a substance that contains carbon, hydrogen and oxygen atoms, such as starch or sugar.
catalyst a substance that starts a reaction or makes it proceed faster but does not actually take part in it.
cell the building block or basic unit of an organism.
composite made from more than one substance.
concrete a substance made from cement, sand, gravel and water.
corrosion a chemical reaction caused by air, water or other chemical on the surface of a metal.
digestion a process by which large molecules are broken down into smaller molecules.
element a substance made up of atoms of just one type.
enzyme a natural catalyst found in cells.
fiber a long thin thread of material.
gas a substance containing molecules that move freely and fill all of the available space.
gel a substance that is part solid and part liquid.
glue a material that will bind two surfaces together.
inert non-reactive, not easily changed.
latex a milky liquid produced by plants.
lignin a woody substance laid down in the cell walls of some plant cells.

liquid a substance with a fixed volume but variable shape.
lubricant a substance, often a liquid, that allows two surfaces to move smoothly over one another.
malleable capable of being shaped by hammering.
mass a measure of how heavy an object is, the quantity of matter.
material the type of matter from which something is made.
metal a substance that has a metallic appearance, is malleable and is a good conductor of heat and electricity.
molecule a group of atoms bonded together.
molten a substance in a liquid state.
mucus a thick gel secreted by membranes.
organic made by living organisms.
plastic useful human-made material made from oil-based chemicals.
polymer a large molecule made from of sub-units.
regeneration regrowth of a new organ or tissue.
resin a sticky substance produced by plants.
rubber an elastic material made from latex.
solid a substance that has a fixed shape that is difficult to change.
solvent a liquid in which a particular substance will dissolve.
stable not easily broken down.
sublimation a change of state direct from solid to gas without passing through the liquid state.
surface tension a molecular force that pulls the surface of a liquid together into the smallest possible area.
tissue a group of similar cells with a particular function.

Answers to the questions

p. 9 Burning wood is a chemical change since the wood reacts with oxygen in the air to form carbon dioxide. Ash is left.

p. 13 Salt and sand are spread on road to lower the freezing point of water so that ice does not form at 0°C (32°F) but at a lower temperature. This means that ice is less likely to form on the road surface.

p. 14 Dry ice sublimes to vapor — which gives a film set or concert stage an eerie or atmospheric feel.

p. 17 Wool will shrink if washed in very hot water. This is because the fibers contract in the hot water — they become shorter.

p. 19 Uses of cotton — thread, upholstery, bandages, parts of the cotton boll are used in paints, shampoo, wallpaper, clear tape, nail polish and even explosives.

p. 21 Items of clothing: jeans made from denim, a tough cotton that wears well. Leotards — made from stretchy human-made fabrics — will stretch to give good fit, can be washed many times without losing shape or color. Sweater — made from wool or wool mix — wool fibers trap a lot of air so that the sweater insulates the body against heat losses. Waterproof jacket — probably made of cotton covered in a synthetic waterproof layer. It stops water from entering but has microscopic pores to allow sweat to pass out so that you do not get too hot and sweaty when you wear the jacket.

p. 22 Biodegradable materials will take longer to break down in winter because the temperature is much colder. There will be fewer bacteria and fungi in the ground. Also the few that are present will work more slowly because of the cold temperature.

p. 25 The wood is piled up in such a way that air can circulate around the wood. This allows the water to evaporate slowly. Seasoning can be speeded up by placing the wood in special kilns.

p. 26 Uses of paper — packaging, wrapping paper, cardboard, diapers, newspapers, magazines and books, paper towels, filter paper.

p. 35 Concrete — bridges and buildings, roads, dams, tunnels.

p. 36 Dog's teeth — large canines to help catch and grip food, pointed teeth to rip food apart. Large, pointed molars to break the meat into pieces that can be swallowed.

p. 38 Cleaning teeth — to remove residue of food that bacteria could feed on. Remains of food supply bacteria with a source of energy that they use to grow and reproduce. They produce an acidic waste material that then attacks the enamel of teeth.

p. 41 Soft tires give much better grip than tires made of a harder rubber compound.

Index

Key words appear in **bold face** type.